Alcoholism And Addiction Cure

The Ultimate Step-by-Step Guide on Alcohol Addiction Treatment

Digital Print House Production

Digital Print House

BE A BETTER YOU

Table of Contents

Introduction

This book contains proven steps and strategies on how to overcome alcoholism through a series of steps that are outlined in the book. On the first part of the book, you will be equipped with the information needed to determine if you, or someone you know, might have an alcohol problem. You will also learn about the dangers and destruction that alcoholism can entail and how it can wreak havoc on your personal life as well as on your body.

You will find details about each step that recovery involves including the realization and acceptance that alcohol is a problem in your life, what to expect when detoxing and going through withdrawals and the all-important steps that will guide you in your pursuit of recovery.

Recovery is a journey, not a destination and with that in mind, there are many helpful hints lined out in each of the seven steps such as finding fun and exciting things that interest you and replacing those things you rid your life of with things that are far better.

Overcoming an alcohol addiction is a process that will not only help you to get and remain clean and sober but to actually be grateful for the problem. Many recovering alcoholics say that they are glad they had the issue for it has led them to a life that is much fuller than a "regular" life would have ever been. May you find that joy and gratefulness once you have embarked in the journey that can change and enrich your life as well!

Thanks again for downloading this book, it is time for a great change!

Chapter 1: What is Alcoholism?

Definition

What is **Alcoholism**? The answer to that question usually depends on who you ask. Alcoholism means different things to different people and groups and guess what? They are all correct.

By definition, alcoholism is an addiction to the consumption of alcohol. Simply put, it is the term coined for when drinking alcohol becomes a problem. In medical terminology, alcoholism is the physical and mental condition that is present when one is addicted to alcohol. The unabashed definition is "Misuse, problem use, abuse, and heavy use refer to improper use of alcohol which may cause physical, social, or moral harm to the drinker." And if you ask someone in the Twelve Step program of Alcoholics Anonymous, you would most likely hear that alcoholism is a disease with physical, mental, emotional, and spiritual dimensions and the only way to be free from the clutches of the disease is total abstinence from alcohol.

Manifestations

The manifestations of alcoholism are quite a lot. Some are extremely obvious and others are not outwardly apparent at all. Within the confines of alcoholism, there are signs that alcohol is being abused and is becoming or already is a problem and there are manifestations that indicate there is an addiction present.

What is the difference between abuse and addiction? Abuse is the improper use of alcohol, which includes drinking for the wrong reasons, drinking for too many reasons, making bad decisions regarding drinking such as drinking while driving and other indications that the consumption of alcohol is beginning to get out of hand.

Addiction is when you are dependent upon alcohol. It is when drinking rules your life and everything done is centered on alcohol. It is the physical and mental dependence on alcohol to make it through each and every day.

Signs that indicate alcohol is being abused

Constantly thinking of having a drink. You may be at work or at school but in your mind you are planning your next drink. Thoughts of having a drink are beginning to become an obsession during this stage, whether you are acting those desires out or not, it is a problem.

- **Making poor choices centered on alcohol.** When you get behind the wheel of the car after having one or too many or actually pop open a beer while driving, it is an indication that alcohol is becoming more important to you than making good, sound decisions.

- **Blacking out.** When you go out drinking and don't remember where you parked the car and it turns out to be in the yard, that is called "blacking out". It is different than simply being drunk. It is a period of time where you have no recollection of the events that happened during your drinking spree. Anything could have happened and oftentimes, it does.

- **Hurting yourself and/or others**. Putting alcohol before the safety of yourself and others is a sign that you are abusing it.

Some who drink become violent and abusive when under the influence. Knowing that someone will possibly or probably get hurt when you indulge and doing so anyway is a big red flag.

- **Legal issues**. If you have been arrested for driving under the influence or have had legal problems resulting from alcohol in any way, your partaking is very possibly escalating to the point of abuse. Writing a hot check to obtain alcohol, physically fighting with someone while under the influence and stealing a six-pack are all examples of activities that can lead to a trip to jail. If you have been arrested due to an alcohol related crime, you are in no uncertain terms abusing alcohol.

- **Medical issues**. Is drinking causing physical effects that you are ignoring because you choose to keep it up? If your liver is giving in, you are not eating right or if your resistance is being lowered due to the fact you are consuming alcohol, you are abusing it.

- **Concern of family and friends**. Once friends and family begin to note any, part or all of the things above, they become concerned. Oftentimes when they begin to voice the concerns of alcohol abuse, it pushes the abuser one way or the other. Some seek treatment or solutions for their desire to drink before it gets full-blown out of hand. Others shrink into themselves, continue to give in to the temptation and proceed down the destructive path towards alcohol addiction.

Indications of Alcohol Addiction

- **Use of alcohol spirals uncontrollably.** When you cannot control your drinking habit and cannot quit, it is considered an addiction. At this point, it is an extremely serious condition that must be stopped. It is said that the path of addiction leads to one of three places: jail, institution or death. There is but one option and that is the road to recovery.

- **Obsession.** You have become completely consumed with a one track mind -- alcohol! You spend your days (and nights) acquiring, consuming and plotting to get more. No longer do any other outside activities matter, friends and family are tossed by the wayside.

- **Withdrawal.** When you do not have alcohol in your system, you feel sick. **Symptoms** may include nausea, fever and even tremors.

- **Medical Conditions.** You begin to suffer from physical ailments due to alcohol such as reddening of the nose and cheeks, gastritis, stomach issues and general poor health.

- **Tolerance.** Your tolerance level changes. You begin to require more alcohol to feel the effects or to keep withdrawals away. While a six-pack used to get you feeling tipsy, it now takes two or three.

Standard Alcohol Drinking versus Alcohol Abuse

There is a fine line separating the distinction between social drinking, alcohol abuse and alcohol addiction. When you are passing from one stage to the next, you hardly notice it until you have already crossed over. That is one thing that makes alcoholism so deceiving. In Alcohol Anonymous (AA), it is referred to as a cunning and baffling disease.

Although alcoholism is an addiction like having a heroin habit is, it's not as forthcoming. While a junkie must go to the dope house and score his fix, an alcoholic merely walks into the local liquor store and leaves with his (or hers). A meth addict certainly wouldn't do a bump in public but an alcoholic can fit right in at any bar, restaurant or company party. It's socially acceptable to drink yet not socially acceptable to be a drunk. Where is the line drawn and how exactly is the line defined?

Because standard, or social, alcohol drinking is so acceptable, many alcoholics have gotten their start by consuming it like others do but one thing led to another and their drinking got out of control. A man who liked to have a few beers with friends or a highball at business lunches may pump his alcohol consumption up a notch when his wife of twenty years walks out of the marriage with his best friend. And who wouldn't? Sometimes a situation that life dishes out is the root of alcohol abuse.

Others seem to be genetically pre-dispositioned for disaster when it comes to alcohol. While some scientists attribute it to actual genes, AA gurus say it all due to the disease of alcoholism and many religious teachings say it is the lot of a sinner. One thing's for certain, some people have a problem with alcohol from the first time it ever touches their tongue.

While some people are content with a drink or two on a social occasion, there are others who take it to the next level. They don't stop with one or two and find that "one is too many and a thousand is never enough." Not only do they overdo the amount of alcohol they consume, they drink too often as well.

We've all witness this in action. Joining in a toast of champagne at a wedding is a social gesture, often followed by a drink or two during the dance and reception. Everyone is happy and joyous and perhaps some are even a little tipsy. Then there seems to always be at least one in the crowd who cannot handle their liquor. They get rowdy, obnoxious and out of control before the night is over. When the rest of the guests have long since put down their drinks, he (or she) is just getting started. The big drinker often says or does things that are not socially acceptable and many times does not even remember doing so once he or she sobers up. For these people, social drinking is far from social and the behavior they display is certainly not acceptable.

When alcohol becomes a problem, it is exactly that -- a problem. Alcohol abuse is using alcohol like a drug. A social, or normal drinker, would not drink because his or her finances are in disarray. They would most likely find that to be a reason not to drink for it costs money. An alcohol abuser, on the other hand, will find lack of finances to be a reason to drink even more. Likewise, a normal drinker would not continue to drink if his or her spouse threatened to divorce him or her if they did so. But an alcohol abuser will drink although there are extreme reasons not to.

When a social drinker crosses over to abusing alcohol, the chances of him or her becoming an alcoholic is very great. It generally takes a bottoming out of sorts to jolt him or her back to reality and to give up drinking. When that line is crossed and the person is unwilling to quit, he or she is usually nearing the stage where they are drinking so much on a regular basis that their body becomes physically addicted.

Then, not only has the line between social drinking and alcohol abuse been crossed but the line between alcohol abuse and alcohol addiction has been crossed as well. This is when, if there is no change, there is sure to be disaster.

Oftentimes there is denial that comes along with the problems of abuse or addiction so it is common that it will take an awakening in order to stop the madness. The awakening may come in the form of a trip to jail, killing someone in a car wreck while drunk or simply reaching the pits of despair. Sometimes, it is an intervention of family and friends that gets the recovery process started. Oftentimes, the alcoholic refuses to seek help regardless of consequences, confrontation or any other condition and ends up in a jail or prison system, mental institution or dead.

According to the National Institute on Alcohol Abuse and Alcoholism, content varies with the type of Alcohol such as wine, beer, or malt liquor. Regular beers have 5% alcohol content whereas several light beers have 4.2%. In the United States, a standard drink includes 14 grams of pure alcohol seen in 5 ounces of wine with a 12% alcohol, 12 ounces of regular beer, and 1.5 ounces of distilled spirits which contains approximately 40% alcohol content.

Maybe you wonder how you will know that you already have too much. There are markers that can serve as basis for one **"Standard Drink"**. A 12 fl. ounces of regular beer with 5% alcohol is one. Another instance is drinking 5 fl. ounces of 12 % alcohol content Table Wine which is equal to an 8-9 fl. ounces of malt liquor having a 7% alcohol concentration. Lastly, 1.5 fl. ounces shots of 80 poof spirits such as vodkas, whiskeys, tequilas, rums, or gins with a 40% alcohol content is still considered a Standard drink.

Chapter 2: Effects of Alcohol

What Happens to your Brain and Body when Drinking Alcohol?

While having a small glass of red wine to relax in the evening is said to be good for your heart, drinking excessively or too frequently is not. Not only does the overconsumption of alcohol cause potential problems to arise on a personal level, but it also leads a way to many physical issues as well. The effects that alcohol has on the brain and the body in just one night of partying are astounding. The effects of saturating the brain and body with it over a period of time can be grave.

Alcohol's Effect on the Brain. Alcohol is made of ethanol, a neurotoxic psychoactive drug. Sound scary? Well, it is. Although alcohol has been used in beverages for recreational, social and medicinal reasons throughout history, it is actually quite dangerous to the body.

Alcohol, or ethanol, is a depressant. It suppresses the central nervous system, which means it slows down the rate in which the brain functions. Neurotransmission levels are greatly decreased when alcohol is present in the brain. Stimulation and arousal are also depressed, meaning the activity of the brain is not working at full speed. When you are driving with alcohol in your system and see an oncoming car, your brain does not react with the speed and clarity it does when you are sober. The greater the percent of blood alcohol content you have in your system, the slower and more distorted your brain perceives things, including danger.

Alcohol not only depresses and slows down the communication the brain has through the pathways, it actually disrupts and alters the signals. When out on a night of heavy drinking, you might suddenly become enraged because your spouse hugged an old friend. You might have beat one or both of them up but the truth was that the display of affection was actually quite clean and above suspicion which you would have never thought anything about under normal circumstances. Likewise, you might be driving and think the car in front of you came to a screeching halt so you do the same, causing a massive car pile-up behind you. Things are not seen in reality when under the influence including physical sight and emotional and mental perception as well.

Have you ever been asked to do a Sobriety Field Test? If you have, then you know the officer will ask you to do a number of physical coordination exercises to determine if your blood alcohol content is over the legal limit. The way in which it is obvious if it is lies in the fact that your brain does not perform activities clearly. It inhibits your ability to do simple tasks such as to walk in a straight line or touch your nose.

If you think the effects alcohol has on the brain during a night of indulgence is frightful, consider what happens over a period of time when alcohol is consumed regularly. Alcohol disrupts the brain and its tissue as mentioned above. When this happens over an extended period of time, it actually shrinks the brain because it alters and changes the neurons which are the electrically charged cells responsible for transmitting information from the brain to the rest of the body.

Although excessive, long-term alcohol consumption causes the brains shell, or cavity, to grow larger, it has the complete opposite effect on the actual brain mass. When the brain size is reduced, so is its ability to perform functions such as motor skill coordination, remembering, sleeping, regulating moods, learning, conception and a host of other tasks.

Taking a look at individual areas of the brain and how they are affected by long-term alcohol use. The cerebellum is the part that is responsible for motor coordination. When it is impaired, balance is also lost. That is why drunken individuals stumble around a lot. Have you ever experience tumbling down a flight of stairs or been unable to walk properly after a round of drinks? Your cerebellum is the area of the brain that causes that reaction after a certain limit of alcohol is reached in one night and so much more so over an extended period of time.

The cerebellum also controls the brain's emotional and memory responses. Someone under the influence of alcohol is much more likely to get sad, angry or ecstatic. It is also common to black-out or not remember what went on during this time. This area of the brain is not only distorted during a one-time round of drinks, but is severely impaired when alcohol is present in the body over a long time frame.

The limbic system in the brain also directly affects memory and emotion. Whether it is one episode of drinking or a long stretch of alcohol consumption, alcohol suppresses its ability to function properly. Becoming forgetful, depressed and being emotionally unstable in general are all symptoms of alcohol's effect on the limbic system.

When you solve a mathematical problem, plan the week ahead or perform your duties at your job, it is your cerebral cortex that allows you to do so. The cerebral cortex has the very important function of enabling your thinking and planning process. It is also the place in the brain that connects to the remainder of the nervous system. It directly causes you to be able to, or not be able to, learn, solve problems and remember things. In addition, it gives the orders on how you react in social situations and how you interact with others. You can imagine the havoc wreaked when this area is impaired during a night of heavy drinking, let alone over an extended period of time.

Moreover, it has been discovered that about 80 percent of alcoholics have a Thiamine Deficiency. Thiamine is also known as vitamin B1 which is crucial for the nerves, brain and muscles to perform correctly. A lack in thiamine can result in serious brain disorders among other things. Such conditions as **Wernicke-Korsakoff syndrome** are not uncommon with alcoholics and are debilitating and chronic.

Drinking during pregnancy has a profound effect on the development of the baby within. It can cause brain damage, Fetal Alcohol Syndrome (FAS) and worst, miscarriage or stillbirth. It is not unknown that alcohol is a teratogenic substance which can harm not only the unborn baby but the mother as well. If not miscarried, the baby will be born with several defects such as having a cleft lip or palate, Central Nervous System damage, anatomical defects, FAS as mentioned above, and a lot more. Remember that even a small amount of alcohol taken during pregnancy does have great effects.

Underage drinkers are at an even bigger risk than adults for permanent and long-lasting brain conditions because their brains are still developing and are more susceptible to serious side effects.

There is a multitude of ways in which alcohol affects the brain. Alcohol impairs and distorts the way in which the brain functions on a number of levels, interferes with new brain cell growth and development.

Alcohol's Effect on the Heart. As you might guess, alcohol is hard on the heart. Heart damage can be brought about by drinking excessively one single time or by an accumulation of alcohol built-up over a period of time. Although studies show that drinking moderate amounts, like a small glass of red wine at bedtime, may actually help to prevent coronary heart disease, alcohol is certainly not beneficial in excess.

High blood pressure is one symptom that is of concern where alcohol negatively impacts the heart. Research has proven that partaking in more than two drinks in any given sitting can very well raise your blood pressure.

For those who already suffer from hypertension, a spike in blood pressure can lead to Stroke, medically termed as **Cerebrovascular Accident (CVA)**. Alcohol consumption can also cause heart failure and strokes even in those who do not suffer from a heart condition or hypertension. It can also be the culprit behind cardiac arrhythmia, cardiomyopathy and even sudden cardiac death.

When alcohol is consumed, especially in excess, there is a great possibility that it will raise the fat levels (lipid) in the blood which are called Triglycerides. Alcohol slows down its rate as well. It is absorbed rapidly and then digested. Because alcohol is made of simple sugars that contain no actual nutrients, it causes a spike in triglyceride levels and can contribute to the liver producing more fats because of this.

Alcohol in the bloodstream can also cause **Atrial Fibrillation,** which is a condition where the heart beats irregularly (known as *Cardiac Arrhythmia*). It actually quivers due to the blood not flushing out properly from the two upper chambers within the heart. Blood should pump from the chambers into the ventricles and when it fails to do so, has a tendency to clot or clump which can easily cause Stroke.

Indeed, a little alcohol might do your heart some good but again, there is that fine line that when crossed, sets the scene for disaster.

Alcohol's Effect on the Liver: While you may never have thought about alcohol's effect on the heart or brain, chances are pretty good that you have at least heard how it tears up the liver. Alcohol and the liver are not compatible in any form or fashion.

To get a better understanding of why the liver and alcohol do not mix well together, it's important to know a little more about the liver and its functions. The liver is the next to the largest organ of the body. It is responsible for getting rid of harmful substances from the bloodstream. The liver also performs the task of changing food and drink into nutrients and energy to be used by the body.

When alcohol makes its way into the liver, the liver is presented with the job of removing it from your body since it has no nutritional value. During this process, it can face serious damage if the alcohol content it is dealing with is more than it can bear. Just like any vital organ, it can get tired of working as well.

Fatty liver, or **Hepatic Steatosis**, is a common liver problem found in alcoholics, wherein the triglycerides accumulate in the liver tissue. Oftentimes, this brings about inflammation of the liver and other problems such as the decrease of the enzymes that fight oxidation. Oxidation is the result of free radical damage and is present in such things as the rust on a weathered bicycle or the browning of a sliced apple. If oxidation sets in, the destruction takes over, growing like a cancer.

Hepatitis is another medical condition that excessive alcohol consumption can cause within the liver. It occurs when the liver is inflamed and a number of other symptoms are present. Decreased liver function, fluid in the cavity of the abdomen, fatigue, jaundice and malfunctioning of the brain due to failure of the liver are all signs and symptoms of alcohol-induced hepatitis.

Liver Fibrosis is another condition that can result from alcohol abuse. It is an over-abundance of extracellular matrix proteins like collagen that causes the malady. Scaring and disruption of the liver are among the issues accompanying the disease. Abnormal cells give way to nodules that are actually results of the attempt of regeneration of cells. In an attempt to give life to new cells and to reform damaged cells because the liver is dying, an accumulation of fibrous scar tissues develop and thus, fibrosis of the liver is born. The scar tissue eventually becomes rock hard and interferes with the metabolic function of the liver.

Liver Cirrhosis is yet another condition seen with alcoholics. It occurs when the fibrosis of the liver reaches a more severe level. Symptoms include fatigue, jaundice, bruising, weight loss and loss of appetite. Cirrhosis of the liver can be very serious, painful and deadly.

The above conditions are some of the ways in which alcohol can affect the liver. Other issues, like **Cancer of the Liver**, can occur as well. There is no set measurement of alcohol that determines when damage to the liver will take place nor is there a certain length of time. It can happen early on or not at all. Some are more susceptible and experience symptoms of liver problems in a short time and with a lower amount of alcohol intake. Others don't see symptoms for a good while and a lucky few alcohol abusers never see liver damage.

The effect of Alcohol on the Pancreas: The pancreas has a pretty big job within the body. It manufactures the chemicals, like insulin and glucagons, which are needed to keep blood sugar on track and that aid in properly digesting food. Located behind the stomach, it is an important part of the exocrine and the endocrine systems so it also plays a role in regulating hormones as well as other substances. You can imagine the trauma the body goes through when the pancreas is not working right.

When alcohol is present within the body, the pancreas produces toxic substances that can cause a world of trouble. One of the medical conditions that can result is **Pancreatitis** which occurs when inflammation sets in and the enzymes that are produced to aid in digestion are released prematurely into the small intestine and therefore damages the pancreas.

Pancreatitis can be acute (short term) or chronic (long term). Acute cases may be limited to a relatively quick bout of extreme discomfort and minimal damage but chronic cases can cause extensive damage to the tissue and vital organs such as the heart, lungs and kidneys as well as the pancreas. There can also be bleeding in the glands. Vomiting, acute pain that is sometimes localized in the back and jaundice are among the symptoms of the disease.

While pancreatitis is the most common condition that alcohol can impose upon the pancreas, there are others that can occur as well. **Pancreatic cancer** can also be caused by alcohol intake. Alcohol can also play a part in the wearing out of the pancreas insulin production that leads to Diabetes. There is no doubt that alcohol stresses the pancreas whether diseases results or not and there is also no gauge of when or if it will happen. Like liver damage, pancreatic damage from alcohol can occur at any time and at any degree.

The role alcohol can play in causing cancer. Cancer is a general term given to more than 100 diseases. In short, it happens when damaged cells spiral out of control and wreak havoc on the body, oftentimes resulting in serious medical problems including death.

The human body is composed of living cells that live, die and reproduce. They keep the tissues and organs of the body working properly and even repair injuries and fight diseases away. The problem comes with some of the cells which do not die but rather grow abnormally and out of control, invading tissues and other parts of the body.

What sets cancer cells apart from other cells, healthy or damaged, is that cancer cells actually change their DNA which is the programming of the cell. Because of this, the cell begins to reproduce other cells that are damaged and out of control. Cancer cells can cause tumors and can also spread throughout the body.

Cancer cells stem from damaged cells. Free radical cells are those that have been damaged and are missing an electron. Since all cells must have two electrons in order to live, these damaged cells set out on a course to acquire their missing electron at any cost which means they will rob a healthy cell to steal one. When that happens, the cells whose electron has been robbed becomes a damaged cell and it sets out to steal or acquire an electron, thus creating a vicious circle.

Free radical cells can be caused by many things. Over-exposure to UV rays can damage cells and that is why it is said that the sun can cause cancer. Toxins that are introduced into the body can cause cell damage as well, like cigarette smoke which can also cause cancer. But you may have never thought about the possibility of alcohol causing cancer but since it definitely damages cells, it certainly can and does.

Here are some of the most common cancers that alcohol can cause:

- **Mouth**. Alcohol is one of the leading culprits of mouth cancer. Because alcohol is introduced into the body by way of the mouth, it can cause damage to cells within the mouth and those damaged cells can turn into cancer cells.

  Signs and symptoms that accompany mouth cancer can easily be mistaken for typical oral problems such as gum distress or common dental issues. That makes cancer of the mouth even more dangerous since early detection is key factor in successfully combating it.

  If you have a sore that will not heal on your lip or in your mouth, it could be a sign of cancer. Loose teeth, swelling or thickening within the mouth, bleeding of the gums or any other area of your mouth and soreness in the back of your mouth or throat area can all be warning signs.

- **Esophagus.** When drinking alcohol, it travels down the esophagus, so just as with the mouth, the cells it encounters along the way are at risk for becoming damaged and ultimately turning into cancer cells.

  Upon introduction into the body, alcohol is metabolized into acetaldehyde which is a toxic chemical. Once it gets further into the body, it is broken down into acetate. The esophagus is one place in which alcohol is in its toxic form when it passes through. Thus, it poses a huge risk for medical issues such as cancer.

Some people are born with a deficiency ALDH-2 which is an enzyme used to process acetaldehyde. When a person with this deficiency drinks alcohol, they tend to flush or redden the face. This condition raises the risk of cancer when alcohol is consumed because acetaldehyde is not processed well and can more easily damaged cells.

An unexplained loss of weight, loss of appetite, difficulty and pain in swallowing, vomiting, nausea, chest or stomach discomfort, diarrhea and bloody stools are all signs and symptoms of esophagus cancer.

- **Throat.** You have probably come into contact with someone who talks through an artificial voice box. Most likely the reason for the device was that they had throat cancer. Throat cancer refers to three areas that can have cancerous tumors: the pharynx (throat), tonsils and the larynx (voice box). Alcohol can greatly increase your chances of throat cancer, especially since it is introduced through the throat which poses much greater problems because alcohol damages cells which can contribute to cancer. The throat, a tube that is muscular in nature, is situated behind your nose and goes to and ends in your neck. The voice box is made of cartilage and houses the vocal cords. It is located right under your throat and therefore affected by drinking as well. The epiglottis is the lid to the windpipe and the tonsils are right in the back of the throat. All of these areas suffer from the introduction of alcohol into the system.

A sore throat, pain in your ear, hoarseness or other changes in your voice, a cough that doesn't go away, a sore or lump that doesn't heal and unexplained weight loss can be signs of throat cancer. Those who drink and smoke or drink and chew are at an even higher risk of this type of cancer.

- **Liver.** Alcohol damages the liver as well as liver cells. When these cells are damaged, they can become cancerous. In addition, acetaldehyde that is produced when the liver breaks down ethanol (alcohol), abides in a greater volume when excess alcohol is consumed. That makes it very difficult and sometimes impossible for the liver to eliminate it all which also makes the risk of cancer greater due to alcohol. Preceding conditions that are often brought on by alcohol abuse, such as cirrhosis of the liver or fatty liver, can increase the chances of liver cancer.

The liver filters out the blood so cancer of the liver is indeed a serious condition. Signs and symptoms may be so subtle that you don't even notice them. An unexplained drop in weight and/or loss of appetite is the main symptom of liver cancer.

- **Breast.** The risk of breast cancer is increased with the use of alcohol. It damages DNA in cells and can cause cancer to surface anywhere within the body. The breast is one of the most common types of cancer. Alcohol also can elevate the levels of estrogen and various hormones that can contribute to breast cancer. The number one sign of breast cancer is a lump within the breast tissue. Studies have shown that women who indulge in alcohol three times a week have a 15%

greater breast cancer risk and that rate goes up another 10% per each additional drink each day.

Alcohol is a carcinogen which means, it is apt to cause cancer. The statistics are alarming. Of all cancer cases in the world, 3.6% are attributed to the intake of alcohol and 3.5% deaths cancer deaths are attributed to it. In this day and age with all the toxins in the air we breathe and the chemicals in the foods we eat, the risk of getting cancer is great enough, adding excessive alcohol consumption to this risk list just doesn't seem like a smart gamble.

Alcohol and the Immune System:

Have you heard that abusing alcohol weakens your immune system? And if you have, what was your first thought concerning that statement? Most people are inclined to think that having a lower immunity simply implies that they will be more likely to catch a cold or to get the flu but having a compromised immune system means much more than that.

When your immune system is working at full or at least average force, it wards off all sorts diseases and illnesses. Alcohol, when consumed excessively, impairs your body to where it no longer effectively fights such things and leaves you an easy target for all sorts of medical issues. In fact, studies have proven that your body's immune system actually remains impaired for up to 24 hours after you put on a good drunk so imagine how poorly it works for a person who stays intoxicated much or all of the time.

Alcoholics have elevated levels of immunoglobulin's which are actually antibodies. While that may seem like a good thing, consider autoimmune diseases where the body makes antibodies rather than doing what it should be doing and fighting infections. When antibodies are too excessive, they basically turn on the body as with Lupus, Grave's Disease and many other autoimmune diseases.

Cytokine imbalance is another way in which alcohol affects the immune system. When an alcoholic has an unhealthy and diseased liver, the monocytes within the bloodstream and the fixed macrophages produce too much pro-inflammatory cytokines which can lead to very serious issues.

Alcohol also inhibits the activity of NK, or Natural Killer cells. These cells are vital within the body to defend it against disease and infection. NK cells even play an important role in keeping the body cancer-free.

Pneumonia is an example of a disease that you can catch when your immune system is not functioning efficiently. Tuberculosis is another. So yes, alcohol consumption in excess lowers your body's resistance and can make you more likely to catch a cold or flu but there are a host of other conditions it may lead to as well.

Complications of Taking Too Much

Consuming too much alcohol, at best, can have unwanted consequences on the body. At worst, it can lead to debilitating, serious conditions such as death. Alcohol is a depressant. It slows down the central nervous system and depresses the nerves. Meaning, breathing is done at a lower rate and gagging is as well.

If too much alcohol is consumed during a period of time, you can quit breathing all together and also, you may choke because of the failure of your gag reflex to prevent it. Another dangerous fatal scenario is that you can choke on your own vomit since too much alcohol often causes one to throw-up and if you are unconscious due to the amount of alcohol you have taken in, you can asphyxiate.

The tricky thing about blood alcohol concentration (BAC) is that it can continue to rise even though you have stopped drinking or even if you are passed out cold. That puts an end to the belief that you can sleep off a drunken night. Don't bother brewing up a cup of strong coffee to sober up for that does not work either. The only cure for a BAC that is too high is time and that is something you may or may not have. When the BAC in you is too high, you may have blood alcohol poisoning.

Here are some Symptoms of Alcohol Poisoning:

- Vomiting

- Mental confusion, coma and unconsciousness

- Seizures

- Slow and irregular breathing

- Hypothermia

It is imperative that the person suspected of having alcohol poisoning to be given proper medical attention to preserve life. Even if death does not occur, the chances are there that brain damage will occur.

Alcohol is truly cunning and baffling. Most people who partake in a drink occasionally don't consider the possibility that in doing so, they could possibly pick up a drinking habit, given the right (or wrong) circumstances. You doubtfully have worried about alcohol poisoning when you were sauced or given throat cancer a second thought as you pop the top on your favorite brew. While those scenarios are extreme, they are not as uncommon as you might think so the next time you go to take a drink, you might want to think again.

Chapter 3: Common Reasons for Drinking Alcohol

Ask any alcoholic the reason of his or her habit and he or she will probably have a list of reasons, some legitimate, some not. Alcoholics are notorious for making excuses and justifying behaviors because it minimalizes the problem or at least to them it does.

When it comes to why an alcoholic drinks, there are reasons and then there are excuses. There is a difference. While no reason is a good one, it is a reason all the same and can help explain underlying factors and can even aid in finding solutions as well.

There are those who become alcoholics almost innocently. They don't set about an intentional course to become dependent on alcohol, it just happens. One who drinks frequently over a period of time may be developing a tolerance for and a dependence on alcohol and can be doing so unaware that they are.

Here are some of the most prevalent reasons people drink:

- **Depression.** One of the most popular reasons behind drinking is depression. A person who feels sad, lonely or down is apt to seek relief from the pain. Depression can be short term or long term. Those with mental health issues like bipolar disorder are susceptible to drinking especially when they are down. Individuals who are going through an especially hard time such as the loss of a loved one, a divorce or even a period of unemployment can lean on alcohol to pull them through rough times. There are many reasons that people can become depressed and various lengths of time they may do so and using alcohol is a common escape used by all.

- **Age.** A young person who drinks can easily end up with problems of dependency. Their bodies are less developed which makes them more susceptible to the power of alcohol. Because their reasoning skills and ability to weigh out consequences, they may very well find themselves in too deep in a short time. Many young people are bent on partying and are not thinking of where it will lead. Because some have little or no responsibilities, the consequences may not show up as quickly as an adult who has a job, family and other things to attend to. Furthermore, the physical effect that alcohol has on a young person is greater because they do not have a tolerance built up as an adult might.

- **Social Drinking.** The consumption of alcohol is not illegal. In fact, it is socially acceptable in many cases which may make it possibly more dangerous than illicit drugs. It is considered relaxing and glamorous to have a drink whereas it is not usually depicted as such to do drugs.

- **Pain.** Whether dealing with the physical, mental or emotional type, pain is a leading reason people drink. For chronic physical pain management, while it's not a realistic viable option, alcohol does temporarily numb pain. It does the same for emotional and mental woes too, at least for a short time.

- **Genetics and Family History.** You have probably noticed that alcohol abuse tends to run within certain families.

Alcoholism can be hereditary. One reason is that it is common for those who have grown up in a home where adults drank to drink themselves. If your father had a ritual of coming home from work to a cold beer, you may very likely do the same just as a person whose parents drank at holiday and special events may do so as well. Those who grew up with one or more parents drinking alcohol in excess may end up doing the same.

- Not only do social family dynamics tend to influence behavior, even the genes that we are born with can as well. Some unfortunate souls are born with genes that make it more likely that they will, or will not, become an alcoholic. Some of these genes have to do with nationality. Certain ethnic groups, such as Asians, do not tolerate alcohol well and alcohol actually makes them feel poorly rather than good so they are at less risk, as a whole, than other ethnic groups. On the other hand, some are born preprogrammed for dependency on alcohol and other addictions as well. Much has been learned along these lines in the past decades but there is still much more research in the making. The fact remains though that some people are genetically set up for problems with alcohol and it usually doesn't take long for that condition to manifest itself.

- **Mixing alcohol and prescriptions.** Even when done unintentionally, the mixing of drugs and alcohol can quickly lead to alcohol abuse. The combination can create an effect that elevates the toxic effects of alcohol and can therefore make the "high" more desirable which can cause an addiction.

The combination can also increase the potency of alcohol so the physical addiction can rear its ugly head more quickly and severely.

- No matter why a person drinks, when he or she does so regularly and over an extended stretch of time, it is very possible that he or she will develop a dependency problem. Those who binge, or go on sprees where they drink heavily, are at risk as well. While there are always reasons and excuses to drink, there are always even more reasons not to.

Chapter 4: Alcohol Addiction Treatment: Self-help

In the Alcoholics Anonymous Program, there are 12 Steps of Recovery. In some religious-based programs, there is but one which is to surrender to a Higher Power. There are many avenues to recovery, each with their own road map and most, if not all, of them are right on the money. These Seven Steps are in no way meant to take the place of or undermine any of the blueprints other recovery organizations have adopted. In fact, these steps go right along with the most. By taking each of the Seven Steps below, you can overcome addiction and experience life at its fullest.

STEP ONE. Realizing and Admitting the Problem. After reading the information in this book so far, if you believe that you, or someone you know, have an alcohol problem, the first step of recovery is to admit it. No matter if you lean to the traditions of AA, a religious-based philosophy, alternative beliefs or whatever approach you may be partial to, if any at all, the first step will always be to see and admit that you have a problem. Then, and only then, treatment can begin.

Whether you have known there was a problem of great magnitude before or if you are just now really taking it to heart and realizing that there is, consider this your wake-up call. Don't despair though; many are not fortunate enough to get a warning. This is the chance of a lifetime to turn your life around!

STEP TWO. Come to the Conclusion that the Problem is Bigger than You. So many alcoholics and addicts, in general, feel that they have the bull by the horn. Remember, though, that alcoholism is a cunning and baffling disease. It entails thoughts of grandeur where you feel you are on top of the world and times of great despair as well. Keeping in touch with reality is hard to do when your thinking is impaired. Remember the effects of alcohol on the brain?

It is when you come to grips with the reality that your drinking problem is out of control and that your life has become unmanageable that you can finally surrender to the concept of overcoming. Have you ever rescued someone who was drowning? The natural thing to do if you are the one drowning is to fight with all your might. Of course this only makes it more difficult, and sometimes impossible, to save the person. There are times when the person who was drowning had to be knocked out in order to keep them from fighting the one trying to save them so they could be rescued. The same is true when it comes to alcoholism. The quicker you give up the fight, surrender and realize that you are in over your head, the quicker you can experience freedom from the disease.

STEP THREE. Give in to The Solution. "The Solution" is different for each people. What works for Boy A may not work for Boy B. While one may find the God of the Bible as "The Solution", another may find solace in the teachings of Buddha. Others may find salvation within a group of other recovering alcoholics. Still others may find the key to their recovery is a series of self-help steps. Regardless of what solution you find, the most important thing is to search until you find one that is right for you. It is out there. For every problem there is always a solution.

STEP FOUR. Set Goals and Get Excited about the Change. Excitement motivates! Even in your darkest hour of despair, know that there is a light at the end of the tunnel, that your life is going to change and that it is going to be a great one. Most people who are in recovery say that their life is better for having gone through the experience of addiction so they could experience recovery and a quality of life they may not have achieved if their life had been "normal". "I would not trade my addiction for normal life even if I could," expressed one recovering addict. "It has made me who I am and…I like who I am."

Set clear cut goals in order to get to where you want to be. Baby steps are best although most addicts and alcoholics would rather go from point A to point Z in one step; it is just not practical and usually not possible. Start with the steps you will need to take to get completely clean from alcohol. If you do not intend to complete refrain from alcohol, that is your choice and you can list the steps you will need to take in order to cut down or whatever your goal is but be advised that if you are truly an alcoholic, you cannot manage drinking and to be free from the clutches of its addiction, you will need to completely refrain.

Included in your step toward the goal of getting clean and sober should be a clear cut plan of how to do so safely. Alcohol is addicting and detoxifying might not suit one well. The next chapter is devoted in part to detoxifying so you may want to go back to that step after reading it. Nevertheless, you can list the steps, including getting detoxed, and underneath each of the steps, list the smaller steps that you will need to take.

If your goal is to get clean, you may list get clean as the first goal. Under that goal, you may write out get rid of alcohol around the house, quit hanging with those who drink and detox. Under each of those, you can jot down anything you may need to do in order to make those things happen such as blocking phone calls from those who party too much.

After you have listed the steps you will need to take in order to achieve the goal of getting sober, you can continue the list. After getting clean, a whole new future is possible. What are your long term goals? For those whose alcoholism has led to losing custody of a child, you may want to pursue the process of regaining custody if that is possible. Others may be in financial ruin due to alcoholism and may wish to repair their credit, find a better job and so forth. Also list fun and exciting things you would like to do like write a book, run a marathon, and help other addicts or whatever ambition you have.

STEP FIVE. Find a New Way of Life. It may seem impossible to conceive that your life will be reborn but it will be. Your slate will be wiped clean and you will have a fresh new start. Perhaps you can't even "go there" until you have completed the steps above and have gotten clean and are feeling better physically and mentally but when you are ready, this step is empowering.

In setting goals, you will want to set plenty for your new life. They don't have to be big ones. Just be sure to have some things to work for and look forward to. Things like taking time to read a book or treat yourself to a spa are example of goals that may not seem conducive but they are.

Set boundaries to protect your sobriety. Think of having a dog that you really love who once took off and got lost. You have finally found your long lost dog and never want him to get lost again. What do you do? You contain him in a fenced yard or keep him in the house. You do whatever you have to do to make sure you will never lose him again. Don't you deserve the same?

In setting boundaries, determine your triggers. If being alone on a Friday night is depressing to you and makes you want to drink like you used to do on Friday nights, make plans ahead of time which doesn't include alcohol. If being in a certain setting makes you want to drink, stay away from the temptation and distract yourself. This will require a lot of soul searching and self-honesty but you can do it and will reap the rewards that safeguarding your sobriety brings.

Remember to replace things that you take away. If you used to go get a drink after work, you can stop off for a yogurt or coffee instead. Perhaps you went to a club on the week-ends and had a lot of people you knew there. It may be a good idea to join a group like a recovery group that you can attend on week-ends and meet new friends at. Don't just take things away; replace them with things that are even better.

STEP SIX. Prepare For Temptation. The best way to avoid a relapse is to prepare for it ahead of time. You will encounter temptation. That is a given unless you are a rare minority.

Temptation is only temptation though and does not have to lead to drinking but in order to assure that is all that it is, you need an escape plan.

What you put into your head, you are likely to do. If you do not have anything planted and etched in your head, there is no telling what you will do. You will be tossed like the wind and will either relapse or not, it is anyone's guess if it is dependent on a decision you make in the heat of the moment. But if you determine in your mind that you will not, under any circumstance, give in to temptation, the score is settled.

Now, plan even further. What is your escape plan? Firemen urge families to have an escape plan in case their house catches on fire. They say it is actually good to have several in case one fails. You may plan to go out the front door but if the fire is in front of it, you may have to go through a window. Calling someone you trust is a good plan to implement when faced with temptation. But what if he or she is not home? You may have a second person you can call or you may opt to go to a recovery meeting, church or wherever you find solace.

Removing yourself from the temptation is another great plan to precede the act of calling someone or going somewhere safe. Think of what you would do if your house was on fire. You would get out. In the event of temptation, your house is on fire. All you have worked for and all the hopes and dreams you have for your life are at stake so have an escape route that is foolproof.

STEP SEVEN. Progress in Your Sober Life. Recovery is a journey, not a destination. There are things you will need to do in order to assure that you keep growing and evolving in your new life.

- **Do something towards your recovery every day.** In recovery, if you are not going forward, you are going backwards. Remember where you came from and know what it takes to keep from going back. Read recovery material and feed your spiritual side. Socialize with other recovering alcoholics or with a group of some kind that encourages you in your new walk. Have someone who you trust to talk to. Secrets are like poison, especially to someone with an addiction so be sure to communicate freely with someone who you trust and respect. If you can, it is a great idea to do as many of those things as possible each day but if nothing else, be sure to do at least one of them.

- **Take good care of yourself.** You cannot help anyone, even yourself, unless you are in shape to do so. It is important to eat healthy, get plenty of exercise, surround yourself with good people, make friends and pursue interests and by all means, get plenty of sleep. Don't get too hungry, lonely or tired or you will burn out. Treat yourself as you would someone you love and determine to love yourself.

- **Surround yourself with support.** Figure out which people in your life are positive influences and stick with them. Hang around with those who encourage your sobriety. Find a group of people who you can be accountable to and with whom you can be transparent with.

- **Find new ways to deal with problems.** If you drank when you were under stress, it is important that you deal with stress in a whole new way. Stress will always be part of our lives but the way in which you handle it can change. Consider working out or doing Yoga to relieve stress. Anger is an issue many alcoholics have trouble dealing with. Find new ways to practice anger management such as taking up boxing or a physical sport or join a class that will teach you to deal with your anger in constructive ways. Whatever your life issues are, find solutions that are better than the ones you employed before.

- **Find new interests and activities**. The more excited you are in your life of recovery, the more likely you are to stay on track. You probably spent a lot of time drinking and wasted opportunities to do new things because you were preoccupied with alcohol. Now is your chance to find new and exciting things that are like icing on the cake. Join a karate class, learn to make soap, climb a mountain or take a trip to somewhere you have always wanted to go. Whatever you do, make sure it is fun and meaningful.

As you implement the steps above or whatever steps you have decided to follow, such as the 12 Steps of AA or any other recovery planned steps, you can also treat your addiction with some additional self-help.

- **Yoga and meditation are great to implement**. They can help your body stay healthy and can ease your stress level. You can enroll in a class or purchase a DVD and do the lessons in the privacy of your own home.

- **Alternative treatments are available as well.** Essential oils, herbal remedies and acupuncture are among the non-traditional options that are available which may help you in your recovery.

- **Hypnotism** is also a popular source for assistance in recovery. You may want to consider working with a hypnotherapist to resolve issues regarding your alcohol use and other factors that played a part in your addiction such as stress, anger, abuse or any other life issue.

Chapter 5: Alcohol Addiction Treatment: Professional Help

Detoxification

If you go to a treatment facility to get sober, you will be detoxed. It is the first thing that will take place. It is imperative to detox your body from the alcohol and doing so in a secure setting is advised. Alcohol detoxification is a very serious matter and if possible, it is best done with medical supervision.

It will depend on how extensive your alcohol addiction is, how much alcohol you are used to taking in and your body size as well as the frequency and length of time you have been drinking as to how severe withdrawals might be. If you are in a hospital setting, this will be determined by the staff most likely.

Detox will be accompanied by withdrawal. Chapter 7 is devoted to withdrawal so you can refer to it to learn even more about what to expect. In general, the process will take anywhere from two to seven days, sometimes shorter, sometimes longer.

Medication for Alcoholism

During your detoxification, you may be given medications to help you along in the process. Usually the medication given aims to prevent confusion and hallucinations which are not uncommon in withdrawals. You may also be given a sedative to keep you from shaking and having tremors.

After Detox

Detox is merely the first step in a series of recovery based treatment. If you are able to, it is good to seek the support of a treatment center to continue your journey. If it is not possible, you can certainly still stay clean and sober by implementing the steps and doing all of the extra activities advised.

If you have gone to a medical setting for help with your detox, the facility will most likely direct you to a place where you can further recover such as a residential treatment program. Otherwise, they can at least help point you to some helpful groups and resource centers.

Chapter 6: Alcohol Recovery Programs and Support Groups

Alcohol Treatment Programs

There are Alcohol Treatment Programs that are available to help you in your recovery. It is a good idea to place yourself in one after you have gone through detoxifying the alcohol from your system.

Some treatment programs are in-house or residential where you'll stay temporarily. There are many advantages of doing so. You don't have to worry with things such as going to work, figuring out what you are going to eat or what you are going to do because everything is taken cared of for you. You have a structured schedule and minimal responsibilities so you can focus on getting better. Counseling is available in the facility such as individual, group and family sessions. Other classes and activities are part of the program as well like recreation and exercise, life skills classes and oftentimes, job skill lessons. The duration ranges from 30 days (the most common) up to one year.

There are out-patient treatment facilities as well. This type of program works best for those who have obligations that prevent them from going to a residential facility like if you have children and no resource available for them to be tended to for the duration of a residential program or for those who cannot take a leave from work. Generally an out-patient program requires that you attend a class, group or counseling session most every day. You will most likely find an outpatient treatment in a counselor's office, hospital clinic, health department facility or mental health clinic. The length of treatment time varies in this type of program and can last anywhere from a month to a year as well.

Your doctor can help advice you as to what type of treatment is best for you although sometimes life designates one way or the other depending upon your circumstances, finances and other conditions.

What Treatment Entails

During the process, you will be exposed to many new things that are designed to assist you in your recovery.

- **Classes**. Alcohol treatment specialists generally lead the groups and offer extensive wisdom and knowledge. Many people who work in treatment centers are recovering addicts who can share their own journey of recovery.

  Lessons regarding goal setting techniques, self-help classes and one-on-one counseling are things that you can expect to encounter during your stay. There may also be classes that your family and friends can attend which will teach them about your addiction and will offer advice on how to support you. Aftercare plans will be set in order as well.

- **Counseling**. Counseling is a big part of treatment. Some counseling is done in group settings and other sessions, individually. A professional is usually in charge of the sessions which are designed to help you better understand your alcohol problem and other issues that may contribute to it or result from it. Some sessions are usually offered for family members who have been affected or will be affected by your alcohol problem. As a result of your assessment in sessions and in other observations, it may be suggested that your psychological treatment be extended. If you have been a victim of abuse, you may be directed to deal with that issue in separate counseling. If you have a condition such as bi-polar disorder, that will be addressed as well.

- **Medications.** Most treatment centers use some medications within the course of your stay. Some of the drugs that you may be given are for the purpose of preventing relapse. They may be used both in treatment and may be prescribed after you leave treatment as well.

Antabuse (Disulfiram) is one medication that is often given that is helpful in suppressing the compulsion to drink. **Revia, or Naltrexone**, is one that actually blocks the positive feeling associated with drinking so if you were to drink, the feeling would not be the one you euphorically recall. **Acamprosate, Campral**, is also used to fight cravings. Some of the medications given will actually make you sick if you do take a drink. **Vivitrol** is an injectable drug that can be given once a month to combat cravings. It is available in pill form too, but some do best with the once a month set up.

- **Support**. During your stay, you will probably be introduced to a 12-Step Program or something similar. You will be encouraged to build a good support set up for yourself, both in the treatment time and once you leave. Additional aftercare programs and options will be introduced to you. Oftentimes, individual counseling suggestions and additional groups may be advised in addition to an AA group or whatever group is advised for recovery. You may have a secondary issue, like anger and be advised to attend anger management classes and support groups or ones that are geared to help those who have suffered abuse or even grief.

- **Medical**. It is common to encounter physical ailments that are caused by the abuse you put your body through while drinking. Most treatment centers perform tests that will help diagnose any conditions that you may have such as liver disease, high blood pressure, and so on. If you do have such an issue or issues, you will most likely be treated and a plan made for you to continue medical help once you leave the facility. You may be given medication to treat the ailment such as a blood pressure prescription or insulin for diabetes.

- **Spiritual Help**. Seeking spiritual guidance is helpful to many who are in recovery. The concept that a power greater than themselves is often comforting and empowering. This help may come in the form of a group or individual counseling setting or may even be attending church or a Bible study. Research has shown that addicts in recovery are more likely to be successful when they nurture and grow their spiritual side.

Support Groups for Alcoholics

There are support groups that are available to help you in recovery. These are very important to attend regularly once you have detoxed and have gone through treatment and are implementing the steps of your recovery plan.

Groups help in many ways. In alcoholism, it is easy to feel that you are an odd duck but when you go to a group with other alcoholics, you have a sense of belonging. You can use the experiences and wisdom of other members to enrich your own recovery and you can also lean upon members and leaders to work through issues that you will encounter.

Another good thing is that you will meet new friends. You will find that some of your old friendships have to be discontinued because they are not healthy so within your new group, you can find new ones.

It is said that those who commit to a recovery group greatly increase their chance for a successful recovery. It is important to determine to be honest and open with those in your circle and to participate fully. It is advised to "go early and stay late" which means to get involved.

Resources

You can find many resources by checking in the phone book yellow pages under "alcohol treatment" and can find a myriad of resources online as well. If you are having trouble finding things in your area, check with the closest mental health facility and they should be able to direct you.

Alcoholics Anonymous is a group for alcoholism support that focuses on 12 steps of recovery. The groups are located worldwide and it is quite likely you can find one near you. Many treatment programs, both in-house and out-patient, use the concept of this program and encourage attending the group once you have completed your initial treatment.

Mountain Movers is a Christian-based recovery group that has regular meetings. The group is along the lines of AA but caters to a niche group that is more religious in nature.

Teen Challenge is a worldwide Christian residential treatment center. The concept of the organization is not a 12-Step Program but rather a Christ-centered way of life in which it is taught that old things are passed away and all things are new. The faith-based programs are available at different locations for different age groups and genders and some are specifically for families. Most facilities are residential and are for a full year.

National Institute on Alcohol Abuse and Alcoholism is a National organization that provides research and information regarding alcohol and the problems and treatments thereof.

Mental Health and Mental Retardation is a national organization that provides resources for alcohol problems and treatments.

SMART Recovery offers help to those who have issues with alcohol. They have online groups as well as personal ones.

Women for Sobriety, Inc. is a non-profit organization that is helpful in assisting women in overcoming alcoholism.

Chapter 7: Withdrawal from Alcohol

Most alcoholics will experience some form of withdrawal from alcohol. Alcohol is a powerful drug that is arguably more addicting than heroin. When in the confines of a hospital detox setting, it is those who are withdrawing from alcohol that are generally treated with the most precautions. Withdrawal from alcohol can be dangerous and should be treated as such. If you can, detox within a medical setting.

Withdrawing ranges from mild to severe. Remember that once you have made it through the withdrawals, you never have to do so again. It is not a pleasant experience, but it is a necessary one and the good news is that if you never picked up another drink, you can have withdrawing behind you once and for all.

What to expect or at least prepare for when withdrawing:

- You may experience a headache, mild, moderate or even severe.

- You may experience tremors and shaking.

- You may sweat a little or profusely as the toxins and alcohol leave your body.

- You may be sick to your stomach and have nausea or vomiting and may not have much of an appetite.

- It is not uncommon to be restless and to have a good bit of anxiety and even depression.

- You may experience stomach cramps and diarrhea or even constipation.

- It is common to have difficulty sleeping or concentrating, and mind-wandering.

- Elevated heart rate and high blood pressure may take place.

The symptoms of alcohol withdrawal may last only a day or two or may continue up to five days to a full week. During this time, keep in mind that the withdrawals will pass although you may not feel as if they ever will. They actually will and you can begin your journey to your exciting life of recovery.

Prevention

The best prevention for avoiding problems with alcohol-like withdrawal and relapse is to not take that first drink. If you have already done that, the next best prevention is to stop drinking before it can become a problem. Some of the fortunate catch alcoholism before it gets a hold on them and that is a much easier, gentler way to handle it. Even if you do get a grip on alcohol before it gets one on you, it is wise to still pursue a treatment plan such as attending AA or a support group. If you were on your way to addiction, there most likely are underlying addictive traits you have that need to be addressed in order to prevent alcoholism permanently.

Conclusion

Thank you again for downloading this book!

I hope this book was able to help you to access if you do have an alcohol problem and determine a course of action if you do.

The next step is to make a commitment to do whatever it takes to live in victory and recover from the grips of alcohol by taking the Seven Steps that are outlined in this book. I hope that in learning about the steps and other suggestions that can help in your recovery, you are less fearful and more hopeful that you can overcome alcohol addiction and live a purposeful, joyful life as you continue in your exciting new life…the journey of recovery.

Finally, if you enjoyed this book, then I'd like to ask you for a favor, would you be kind enough to leave a review for this book on Amazon? It'd be greatly appreciated!

Thank you and good luck!

Preview of 'Drug Addiction Treatment and Recovery: The Ultimate Step-by-Step Guide to Drug Addiction Treatment'

Chapter 1: Drug Addiction Cure and Recovery: The Beginning of a Change

Drug addiction and recovery is highly misunderstood by a lot of people, including those who engage with the habit, itself. Little did they know that understanding it better can be a great start and a first step to cut it off.

The first thing you need to do is to tear down your own misconceptions and misunderstandings. Do not worry about other people having misunderstandings about addiction--just leave them to it. If you want to recover, it is important that "You" understand addiction and that "You" remove those myths about drug addiction.

Change is never easy but it is up to the person if he or she really wants to cease the habit. A person involved should learn that in order to overcome that kind of situation, he or she should be able to find out where to channel or direct his or her life's situations like stress other than using drugs.

Another key to success from drug addiction is to reflect. Ask yourself if you are ready for this kind of change. Are you ready to give up something that you did all those months or years knowing all the possible consequences it can affect your life?

There are other steps to prepare yourself such as reminding

yourself, once in a while, your reasons for ceasing the habit. Set realistic goals like dates or time. When do you plan to start the change? Think of all the possible effect that prohibited drugs can do to your kids, spouse and even to your career and goals. Be aware that using the drug, itself, can make you do the things you never thought you could do because of the intensity of its effects.

It will also help when you involve your family and friends with your plan. It always makes a difference when you get a support from your loved ones. Or if you can't do it alone, you can always seek the help of a trained Professional or Counselor. They can help you avoid a relapse while assisting you with your struggles.

Quitting your habit is not a magic. It entails self-discipline, patience and commitment because at the end of the day, you know that the only person that can help you get through all of this is "You!"

Chapter 2: Drug Addiction

Do not waste time on drugs! There is a whole wide world that is waiting for you out there! Drugs will hinder you from doing a lot of great things and most of all, it hinders quality family life. Embracing reality and accepting change will:

- **Improve your health.** Do not be afraid of the "withdrawal period." There is no fast or hard way to recover from drug addiction or any kind of addiction, for that matter. The withdrawal period is just a small step to getting rid of drugs completely. After this struggle, you will finally be able to live your life drug free and totally improve your health!

- **Seize life opportunities.** You will be able to do and achieve your dreams and goals and the things that you cannot do before. You can finally work or manage your own business, you can start a whole new career, you can study or begin studying again and you can become a part of your family again!

- **Do new things**. Now that you are on the road to recovery, you will be able to do new things that you have never thought possible. You can take up new sports and hobbies since you are more able to concentrate, you can travel and buy new stuff since you now have more money and you can improve your home since you have money to spare.

- **Have a good relationship.** You will be able to handle relationships better when you are completely over drugs. You will be able to cease the erroneous effects of drugs such as verbal and physical abuse.

There are a lot more benefits of getting over drugs and this is just the beginning. Drug addiction and recovery varies from one person to another. Some can stop in a matter of weeks while others could take months or even years to fully recover. But it does not matter. A drug addict that has accepted his condition and is willing to change for the better and is on the road to recovery. It just needs to be done a few small steps at a time.

What is Drug Addiction?

Before you can finally recover from drug addiction and before you start with any kind of treatment, you will need to fully understand what drug addiction is and what the common types of drug abuse are. A drug addict has a drug of choice; some rely on "Downers", which are drugs with certain chemicals that lowers the mood, whereas, some take the "Uppers", drugs that lift the mood. Knowing all of these will help the addict learn strategies on how to combat drug addiction and recover for life.

Drug addiction is defined as using and abusing prohibited substances. Addiction is taking substances on a regular basis since not being able to do so could result to unpleasant physical and psychological effects. This drug dependence is craving a chemical substance to the point that you are willing to trade your life, your safety, your finances and even your family just to get this drug or chemical into your system. Drug addiction is not as simple as it looks.

It starts with simply taking prohibited or prescription drugs occasionally or casually and then it worsens as you crave for the effects of the drugs more frequently. Finally, you become very persistent and emotional if you are unable to take your drug of choice on a daily basis or a more frequent time period. You are convinced that you are not doing anything wrong and you are not affecting anyone. You might also resist help from others and tell them that you are absolutely fine and can handle yourself well.

Drug addiction is a viscous cycle for some drug addicts. Some realize in one point that they need help and actually start (and sometimes even finish) a program for recovery only to take drugs again and this time they become more and more aggressive.

What these people need is a strong support system that will help them recover completely from drugs. A support system could be anyone who is trained and able to support the recovering addict until he is completely over drugs. A support system could be a friend, a family member, a partner or a professional for as long as he is focused on the complete recovery of the person.

What is Prescription Drug Abuse?

Check out the rest of Drug Addiction Treatment and Recovery: The Ultimate Step-by-Step Guide to Drug Addiction Treatment on here: http://www.amazon.com/dp/B0100J99U2

Made in the USA
Las Vegas, NV
22 July 2021